T.

With Best wishes

Mahmood Jamal

Mahmood Jamal was born in Lucknow, India, in 1948. He came to Britain from Pakistan in 1967.

In 1984 Mahmood Jamal was the recipient of the Minority Rights Group Award for his poetry, translations and critical writings. In the same year he published his first volume of poetry, *Silence Inside a Gun's Mouth*. His poems have been published in the *London Magazine* and broadcast on BBC Radio and he has performed at leading poetry venues in London and around the UK. He has also featured in several anthologies including *New British Poetry* and *Grandchildren of Albion*.

Mahmood Jamal works as an independent producer and writer and has produced several documentary series, notably a series on Islam entitled *Islamic Conversations*. He was also a lead writer on Britain's first Asian soap, *Family Pride,* and wrote and produced the groundbreaking drama *Turning World* for Channel 4 television. Mahmood Jamal has a degree in South Asian Studies from the School of Oriental and African Studies, University of London.

Published Works:

Coins for Charon
(Courtfield Press, London, 1976)

Silence Inside a Gun's Mouth
(Kala Press, London, 1984)

The Penguin Book of Modern Urdu Poetry
(Penguin Books, London, 1986)

Modern Urdu Poetry
(Farida Jamal/Translit, Kuala Lumpur, 1995)

Song of the Flute
(Culture House, London, 2000)

Some of the anthologies in which his poems have appeared:

Angels of Fire
(Chatto and Windus, London, 1986)

Ranters, Ravers and Rhymers
(Collins, London, 1990)

Grandchildren of Albion
(New Departures, Stroud, 1992)

Velocity
(Blacks Spring Press, London, 2003)

Rainbow World
(Hodder Wayland, London, 2003)

Sugar-Coated Pill:
Selected Poems

Mahmood Jamal

WP
BOOKS

First published by Word Power Books, 2006

Word Power Books
43 West Nicolson Street
Edinburgh
Scotland
EH8 9DB

Tel: 0131 662 9112
books@word-power.co.uk
www.word-power.co.uk

Printed and bound in the UK by Digisource Ltd.

ISBN 0-9549185-2-5

To All My Friends
Past, Present and Future.

Contents

Introduction by Angus Calder	xii
Preface by Tom Leonard	xviii
You and 1	26
Asian	28
A Peasant in Bengal	29
Immigrant	30
Swamped	31
Sugar-Coated Pill	32
Silence	33
Apples and Mangoes	35
The Way You Loved Me	37
Remember	38
Whose Word is it Anyway?	40
Liberation Fighter	42
Migrants	44
Against Cliches	46
Objectivity	47
Revival	48
Wedding	50
Two Women (I)	51
Two Women (II)	52
Refugee	53

Candle 54

Outside My Window 55

Morning Star 56

Sitar Player 57

Blind Love 59

Suicide 60

No Comment 61

From Stars:

Freedom 62

Dreaming Stars 63

Falling Stars 64

Broken Star 65

Alien Star 66

Black Star 67

The Sun is Your Flower 68

Ghazal 69

I Saw You Dancing 70

Like the Moon 71

Song 72

Prevention of Terrorism 73

What's it All About? 74

A Child's Prayer 76

Introduction

Mahmood Jamal is an outstanding political poet because he is actually a very fine poet.

Nothing is more depressing for those of us who value poetry as perhaps the most significant of all art forms than to attend a rally, meeting or reading where people proclaim verse which says nothing beyond what everybody present (except, of course, the spies and agents provocateurs usually found at left wing political events) already agrees with - or they wouldn't be there. 'Performance poetry' may sometimes actually vitalise and energise such events, but often does not look much good in print. Such political verse as endures does so because it has the permanent relevance of work which is well-crafted, intelligent, moving and goes beyond statements better made in pamphlets or letters to the press, to generate fresh thoughts or empower vivid images with impressive language.

As George Macbeth, himself a good poet, wrote decades back in his introduction to his excellent anthology, *Poetry 1900 to 1975,* in Longman's avowedly educational *English Series:*

> When a poem is known by heart it can stay in
> the mind for a lifetime and affect every thing that
> happens to a man or woman for good or for
> ill... In the First World War, when asked what
> he was fighting for, Wilfred Owen replied: "The
> English Language." This book will not have
> failed if it makes readers see what Wilfred
> Owen meant.

This may seem parochial. Some of the poetry which lingers most strongly in our minds has been translated from other languages into English. Reverting to the question of politics, from the last century one might mention Brecht's marvellous address 'To Posterity', Neruda's precise assault on 'The United Fruit Co.' and certain 'prison poems' in Turkish by Nazim Hikmet. These will continue to speak, as do, in original English, the diatribes of Byron and Shelley against Tory reaction and Owen's assaults on the war which killed him and millions of other young men, through striking imagery and sentences well crafted and shafted. For instance, read this from August Stramm (1864-1915), another victim of the 'Great War', translated from the German by Michael Hamburger, to be found in *The Penguin Book of First World War Poetry* edited by Jon Silkin (1979):

Battlefield

Yielding clod lulls iron off to sleep
bloods clot the patches where they oozed
rusts crumble
fleshes slime
sucking lusts around decay.
Murder on murder
blinks
in childish eyes.

January 1915

Hamburger is a translator to be trusted. The intensely compressed language here wastes not one word. No conventional rhetoric is employed to convey Stramm's horror and disgust.

1 have mentioned foreign poets and quoted Stramm because Mahmood Jamal is one of the multitude of writers nowadays who deploy English forcibly from the background of another, first, language (African, Asian, Caribbean Creole, Polynesian.) One distinction of his very exciting and moving collection is that he draws into English so elegantly elements of the Urdu poetic tradition of his native North-Western Sub-Continent, in which Mohammad Iqbal is central and the late Faiz Ahmad Faiz stands out as a recent master. See, in his powerful title poem:

You dream of the Sword
1 sing of the Rose petal...

- the Rose being a typical motif in that tradition.
(It recurs in *Sitar Player*).

The brilliant *Apples and Mangoes* ironises upon the
contradictions and paradoxes of our 'multicultural' UK
world and the prevalence of 'post-colonial' posturing
by intellectuals. It is a fact that some very fibrous
varieties of mango are good only for sucking, not
slicing. Some (disappointing) mangoes do indeed have
flesh coloured pale like an apple's. But no cross between
apple and mango exists. And anyone from anywhere
can enjoy either an apple or a mango, or both.
Mahmood Jamal satirises the tendency to make political
and aesthetic discriminations where none are necessary.

Next, we encounter *The Way You Loved Me,* where words
and phrases familiar from 'protest poetry' -'power',
'machine gun fire', 'statement of our struggle'
- are applied to an erotic relationship which, like so
many, involves both yearning and anger. The subtlety
here could only be fully explored in very lengthy
analysis - suffice to say here that it goes beyond that
latterday clich'e the personal is political.' Yet the next
poem, *Remember,* communicates instantly political
points which, expressed so clearly and succinctly,
extend the reader's sense of what it means to be

economically humiliated and racially insulted - ending, however, with optimistic affirmation.

Objectivity - title of another telling item - is the word for what Mahmood Jamal actually achieves in poem after poem which is perfectly poised and rhythmically eloquent. In *Two Women,* for instance, there is sympathy without gush, but with deft and exact social observation. *Liberation Fighter,* very movingly but without localised rhetoric, presents the position of those for whom armed struggle, possibly with fatal results for themselves, is necessary:

> ...death is the friend of those
> who love deeply; so I go fearless.

What it says is as applicable to the Italian Resistance against Nazism as to any present-day struggle.

In its second half this collection changes direction towards Eastern tradition. Restraint and technical poise are still salient. Night and stars provide cryptic yet convincing imagery. One poem specifically evokes the Urdu ghazal form. Iqbal is translated, Faiz is avowedly imitated.

And then the collection ends with two emphatically explicit and topical political poems. This is not such a switch as might be thought. Both Iqbal and Faiz were highly political men... .

This book of genuine poetry is concerned both with the music of words and dire realities of our world where beauty and darkness co-exist, and also love and hate. Of the latter dichotomy, in *No Comment,* Mahmood Jamal has this to say:

> So I must learn to contemplate
> Poetry on a stubborn blank screen
> To pixilate it with phantom loves
> Or smudge it once again with hate
> Is, to say the least, obscene.

The implicit generosity of the statement is coupled with necessary detachment. Here is a master of words possessed of something which we can call 'wisdom'.

© Angus Calder, Edinburgh, 2006.

Preface

It is important that this collection of poetry should appear when it does. Mahmood Jamal has lived in Britain since 1967, having been born in Lucknow in India in 1948. His family, like many Muslim families, thereafter moved to Pakistan and it is as a Pakistani poet, film-maker and translator that Mahmood Jamal was to become known in Britain.

At present Britain is daily poisoned with broadcast and newspaper racism and the whipping-up of mass fear. From Prime Minister down, through Press and electronic media, the Enemy Within has moved from being porn-amassing predatory paedophiles, litter-scattering noisy gypsies, young people on council estates (Yob Culture, as the government would have it), lazy single mothers on benefit, invalidity benefit Scroungers (i.e., the sick, especially those in their fifties and early sixties), illegal immigrants with whom the country is supposed to be awash, teenagers wearing hooded clothes (more Yob Culture) - and now the Muslims, most especially the 'fundamentalist fanatics'. New Labour's ever-rolling policy through the years of Crackdowns and Crusades has at last joined into one. Crusades is now the operative word.

I know exactly what fundamentalism is. I was reared on the stuff. "The blood of martyrs is the seed of

Christians" was one of my religious teacher's favourite, of many favourite, sayings in the daily **RE** lesson I got. If you died a martyr, all your sins would be forgiven at that moment, no matter what they were. Mind you, someone else had to kill you. But getting all your sins forgiven in one go seemed about the only way of being sure of getting to heaven in the sin-laden dire-warnings atmosphere of the RE lessons to assembled adolescents of which I was one. 'Mysticism' was sneeringly dismissed as 'misty schism'. There was one, true, holy and apostolic church. And that was it. The rest were superstitious nonsense: at best misguided, at worst the influence of Satan.

This kind of attitude still flourishes in all fundamentalist outlooks - Christian, Hindu, Muslim, Zionist, Jewish. But only Muslim fundamentalism is presently described by Blair *et al* as 'evil': Christian and Jewish fundamentalism, far from being 'evil', provide too much betimes useful support for Western foreign and domestic policy. Before the destruction of Fallujah a rare glimpse on BBC was given of American soldiers receiving communion before battle, and being lectured on the supposed fact that Fallujah was where they were to do battle with Satan. It is rare for such exposes to occur on the British media - even since that film was shown some six months or more ago, the gaps have been closed.

The most notable silence is on Palestine. To mention any detail of the sufferings of the Palestinians, or the brutality of the Israeli occupying forces, it seems, is to 'foment terrorism'. Only this notion can explain the now total, corrupt complicity of journalists of the electronic and paper media in Britain. There is collective silence at the extinguishing of the Palestinian people's hopes of nationhood and human dignity in ordinary day-to-day living. There are still some avenues to get scattered information through the internet: nothing from British press or broadcasting. I am writing this on July 22nd 2005. Four days ago a fourteen year old Palestinian was shot dead by an Israeli soldier for no apparent reason, to witnesses, while sitting in a car at a West Bank checkpoint. Where was this covered in the British media? Answer: nowhere - of course. It never is. We are treated more and more to the television show trials of those who have committed 'crimes against humanity'. Needless to say, these show trials are of perpetrators of crimes who have been on a side that opposes British and American colonisation. As for the daily construction of a wall twice the width of the Berlin Wall, that cuts through villages, travels for hundreds of miles, blocks people from education, hospitals, their tillable land, their relatives; reduces by another 40-50% that mere 22% of their original land the Palestinians occupied; that annexes East Jerusalem, brings another 30,000 illegal settlers into the compass of Jerusalem and expels 50,000

Palestinians from that same city - of all this, nothing at all. It is quite extraordinary. Nothing at all. No photographs, no programmes, no interviews. And anyone who gets energised about these palpable crimes, it seems, must only be 'a Muslim fanatic'. Such a supposition is indeed racism.

The media are at the moment gearing up for the 'withdrawal' as it is called of the 8,000 illegal settlers in Gaza. The Israeli government is for its own interests constructing a state-of-the-art reporting centre for several thousand reporters to broadcast this worldwide. Like all Jewish settlers throughout the Occupied Territories, these 'settlers' have been funded to excellent accommodation and social amenities, aggressively protected by Israeli soldiers, connected with expensive government-funded top-class roads. Now Sharon, while yesterday for instance assuring settlers in the West Bank settlement of Ariel that their settlement or 'bloc' as he would have these called would soon be increased in size and would be forever a part of Israel - contrary to all international agreements and not reported in Britain needless to say; while his Wall still cuts its inexorable colonising miles through Palestinian land - this Sharon is to be presented in 'The Gaza Withdrawal Media Show', if it goes ahead, as The Statesman Man of Peace taking on his 'right wing' on the one hand and 'Muslim extremists' on the other. It is cynical and preposterous nonsense: but knowing that it is cynical and preposterous nonsense, yet Bush, and Blair, and Jack Straw trot it out as a reasonable view. And complicit journalists relay it. Thousands are to report this withdrawal from the tiny strip of land on a sea-edge of Israel that houses one and a half million mostly refugee Palestinians. The illegal settlers, from Brooklyn or wherever it is that most of them have come from, are each to be rewarded with fine new housing elsewhere and thousands of dollars 'compensation'.

And this, the official script trudges on, is to further the 'road map', to bring about The Peace Process. What about The Justice Process? Without justice, a peace process is only a pacification process. The pacification of the natives, again. That is what is being asked of the natives - the true natives - of Palestine. We have had centuries of 'pacification' by colonisers. It has nothing to do with justice, and nothing to do with peace. Here is merely the wished-for conclusion to another military adventure. In Palestine, it is to be a crushed and hopeless population in a topographic quilt of ghettos under permanent electronic and military surveillance, with perhaps another puppet administration of this completely non-viable entity whose main function will be to root out 'extremism' under its wing and be rewarded with episodic photo opportunities with Western leaders. Or the population can clear off to Jordan. But we won't call that ethnic cleansing.

Does all this reasonable cause for anger justify people blowing themselves up in subways full of people going about their ordinary lives? No, nothing justifies that. As Mahmood says in one of his poems here, *THAT STILL DOESN'T MAKE IT RIGHT.* State terrorism does not justify stateless terrorism. But until state cruelty and brutality and carnage stops, we can only expect more of the stateless kind. That's the unfortunate fact of the matter. When Western leaders rush to photo-opportunity handshakes with a Russian leader whose troops have been using devastating 'akin to a tactical nuclear bomb' fuel-air-explosives in the city of Grozny for instance, is it really so surprising that we have Beslan to follow in its wake? Nothing 'justifies' people taking over a school full of children to blow themselves up, nothing can 'make that right'. But what justified the brutality of the Russian government killing thousands of civilians in Chechnya? Nothing makes that right, either. Not above all a strategic silence.

In 1991, writing about the effects of the first major bombing campaign of Iraq, I wrote in an essay published as a booklet by AK Press, "One would have thought that it might have at least occurred to people that there will be Iraqi survivors, or their descendants, who will feel that if there is any justice in the world, the cities of Britain and America will one day get at least a little of what their citizens were apparently so

indifferent to inflicting on the towns and cities of Iraq."
(See http://www.tomleonard.co.uk/other_publications
/mass_bombing-catechism .shtml) Now that what was
so obvious fourteen years ago has happened - and my
surprise was that it took so long to come about - will the
only response be more state violence abroad, more
surveillance and detentions at home? Probably yes.
Evermore un-dicussed money to the arms industry and
'security', evermore erosion of basic rights to privacy.
Evermore 'management of the language environment',
evermore complicit 'responsible' self-censorship by the
media, evermore from the evangelical Mr Blair about
how he is on the side of 'reason' against 'evil'. The word
'evil' invites people to join with the Western governments
on the side of 'good'. It is Crusader speech.

In a deeply unhealthy, some would say insane, culture
like this, it is refreshing always to turn to art, not to get
away from reality, but to be in a reality where honesty
and integrity of purpose and language can still prevail.
Where the human still has currency as a universal. In a
society saturated with agenda-language for the
purposes of maintaining the position of those in
power, how good to turn to Mahmood Jamal's
collection of poems: here is the simple business
of an intelligent poet making art from his own
culture, making his own way in the world which is all

we can try to do in some kind of peace and sanity. In a book that is being published by the independent Edinburgh bookshop Word Power, I am almost tempted to say, "Welcome to the often-boring world of 'Scottish Literature', Mahmood". We humans on the side of creativity in and out of Art, can only try to go on as best we may despite everything, in any time and place.

You and I

You want to speak of War
I want to speak of Peace

You say Punish
I say Forgive

You speak of God's Wrath
I speak of His Mercy

Your Quran is a Weapon
My Quran is a Gift

You speak of the Muslim brotherhood
I speak of the brotherhood of Man

You like to Warn others
I like to Welcome them

You like to speak of Hell
I like to speak of Heaven

You talk of Lamentation
I talk of Celebration

You worship the Law
I worship the Divine

You want Silence
1 want Music

You want Death
I want Life

You speak of Power
I speak of Love

You search out Evil
I warm to the Good

You dream of the Sword
I sing of the Rose petal

You say the world is a Desert
I say the world is a Garden

You prefer the Plain
I prefer the Adorned

You want to Destroy
I want to Build

You want to go Back
I want to move Forward

You are busy Denying
I am busy Affirming

Yet there might be one thing
on which we see eye to eye

You want Justice
So do I

Asian

I have seen the dawn
approach on monstrous iron wings.

Through the mist of tears
I have seen the hills rise
and the moon
weave its way through clouds
in painful insomnia.

It is you
who have measured everything
who do not know how to cry.

A Peasan in Bengal

My first son died
when the cyclone struck.
I found his body in the rubble.
Here it is under my pillow;
it talks to me when I am lonely.

My second son
drowned in the floods.
I have his shirt to remind me;
it smells of my own sweat.

My wife died
giving birth to my third son.
They brought him back
torn with bullets.
I have no reminders of him;
only the rattle of machine guns
across the river.

Immigrant

Distances
the distance
between me and
myself;
the left behind
and the possibility
and the excluded middle
(most certain
of all)
the I that always
arrives at the wrong place
and stays.

Swamped

These are amazing people,
Let us give the devil his due.
From a small island off the coast of Europe,
came down in their ships
with guns swords and whips;
creating men in their likeness,
making tea and tie
synonymous with respectability.
Destroyed the natives of America
to make room for their exiles, thieves.
Exterminated the Carribs
and created the West Indies.
Left quietly as gentlemen often do
with minimum of fuss
but a lot of loot.
Now we hear they're losing sleep
over a handful of blacks at the bottom of the heap
because their culture is threatened
because they are being SWAMPED.

Sugar-Coated Pill

A clever adversary
does not advertise his intentions.
He will come with a big smile
to show his love; and slogans
that even you would hesitate to shout.
Freedom, Peace and Equality
will never be far from his lips
and he will offer every help
to keep you where you are.
A split soul, a lost language
the poison of gifts
the symptoms of slow penetration.
Fantasies on the screen,
arguments that are 'self evident'
And you feel a romantic fool
for trying to change the world.
"Be my wife, my child
and all shall be well."
Flowers, chocolates, perfumes, gadgets
His subtle armaments; what else
could you ask for
being hopelessly divided
friendless, faceless, full of fears?
And while you man the barricades
in battle dress keeping an eye out for
intruders,
He surprises you with an embrace.
You have been disarmed!

Silence

Let my silence speak out
through these words.
Let it seep through these sounds
imperceptibly
as the air we breathe
permeates our blood.

Let the silence
grow as the words grow denser
thickets, bushes, thorny branches
standing in a windless evening;
silent
brooding darkly of day
passing shadow-like
into the dark.

The silence of deep deserted
eyes
            and pitch black
tears.
The silence of moonlight
over the shanty towns.
The silence
inside a gun's mouth
when the bullet has flown.
The silence
of a child's twisted belly
and his old eyes.

Let my silence speak
as the eloquent silence
Of lovers;
the silence of clouds passing
and black evening hills;
the silence of dew damply
falling over fresh graves.
So the silence
can grow as the noise grows
about us of robots
and demagogic lights
that shriek out on the desolate highways
their neon screams.

So that the dark
can be discovered
So that the silenced
Are not forgotten
Let my silence be loud.

Apples and Mangoes

The exotic fruit
was placed upon the table
and invited comment:
"I prefer to eat apples at home",
said the professor from SOAS
"But when out I like a slice or two
of mango;
That is what it is no doubt?"
"Easy to get hold of these days,"
said the liberal host
who wrote guilt ridden plays about blacks.
"A transplant, I can see
by its shape and colour,
from India on African soil"
remarked the social worker from Battersea.
"A good thing surely
in the cause of internationalism,"
muttered the pale bespectacled revolutionary.
"I like its pink blush, subtle
not too obvious in natural light
tastes nice if eaten late at night,"
Said the artist, adding,
"almost nipple like its eye
where all the juice can be sucked through."
"No! No! It's not one you can suck!"
screamed the professor, hands shaking
with age and anticipation as he picked
the knife. "Surely this is one for slicing."

"Some of these mangoes," said the poet,
"look ok but taste like apples
and are the same colour inside."
"Hmm," said the professor as everyone smiled,
"A cross between an apple and a mango!
Science has indeed made great strides."
"Hmm," added everyone as they had a slice.

The Way You Loved Me

The way you loved me
was a lesson in subversion
and the way I loved you
a consolidation of power.

Staring emptily over the wall
is all that is left of our dream
as broken words trip over the wires
and turn to screams;
the smile becomes an intruder's body
twisted by machine gun fire.

Only if we could
kill each other's fears
instead of slaying our hopes
from day to day!
So that every thing you say
becomes a statement of our struggle
and everything I do defies our separation.

But then again
all this is hardly possible.
In the dim light of our thoughts
contradictions and suspicions multiply.
And we wait for night time
to send us down the streets again

in search of each other.

Remember

Remember when you're out walking
alone in the pale neon of his world
dragging tons of abuse
piled high upon your back.

Remember, brother, when they leave you
stranded, like a gypsy at the gate
of their mansion, with a coin to comfort
their conscience.

Remember, sister, when you're so lonely
that you could tear down the walls
with your teeth and nails.

Remember when you're so angry
that you could burn
like a fire furiously erupting.

Remember, when you can hear the laughter,
that demeaning piercing laughter
when the joke is on you and you feel
like crying.

Remember, bother, when a child
undermines your confidence
by screaming at you
the obscenities that newspapers
relish.

Remember, remember
You are winning.
The Majority of the World.
Not their Minority.

Whose Word is it Anyway?

You said I was free
And I took your word for it.

You said there will be peace
and justice and a new order.

And I took your word for it.

You said it was all a mistake
 that the majority of the world
was subjugated and oppressed.

And 1 took your word for it.

You spoke of stability, security,
a better life for all.

And I took your word for it.

You have thrown so many words at me
that I buckle under the weight of your enormous
sentence.
1 wade through the millions of words piled high,
I try to
catch my breath and find a voice.
I swim in the nuances of your endless tracts,
in the metaphors of violence
in the irony of your phrases.

In your paragraphs of good intentions
I am imprisoned in parentheses
(underdeveloped, dependent, silent)
In your meaningful incantations
I am mere commas and semi-colons.
And you go on insisting that we are free
to speak, to vote, to determine our destiny.

Caught in the web of your language
and the torrent of your definitions,
printed, broadcast, microfilmed, copied,
I resort to silence
I resort to guns
1 resort to action.

Liberation Fighter

Sometimes my back feels heavy,
my machine gun cold as steel
But death is the friend of those
who love deeply; so I go fearless.

Trudging the hillsides with the heavy
tread of my belief,
I struggle to remain hidden
while most yearn to be known.
I am a shadow.
Only my actions are real:
an explosion that rocks a general's sleep,
or a missing foreign soldier.
"My people are my mountains"
and they hide me in their caves.

One day, it may happen
that I will be taken
quietly, stealthily to the riverside
by uniformed men, the general's men
and be destroyed;
without witness without audience.
But they will only destroy a shadow.
No poets will write about me;
but the villagers will remember me
my friends in the chai shop
wondering why I threw
a wall of silence around them.

My body will never be found.

At night, I'll rise with the water
seep down as mist over the valleys.

And when my friends are thirsty,
they will find me glittering in a well.
They will drink me up
and continue the fight.

Migrants

We migrated before we moved,
the gestures that we knew
were sown into new garments;
new words emerged
from our lips.
We learnt to drink
tea from cups
and water in glasses.
Knives and forks
replaced our fingers,
but the cuisine was stubborn
demanding its own etiquette.
Our shoes were laced,
neatly tied up
we were delivered
into service of a new age
despairing of our inheritance.

We read comics, chewed gum
drank coke from bottles,
watched John Wayne shoot Indians
as we clapped.
Then Marylin Monroe smiled,
After shave arrived
Hollywood style.

The radio blasted us with rock and roll
and we learnt to dance
for a dollar or a dime
and signed our future on dotted lines.

We migrated before we moved;
The other place came to us.

Against Clichés

Although death may appear
Black as night
Or dark as a well
Ultimately
It is white as bones.

Objectivity

On a dark night
Only when you turn the light out
In your room
Can you see beyond
the window pane.

Revival

We gave up our past too easily
in exchange for off-the-peg cultures,
made package deals with progress.

Believing that the past was a corpse
half-eaten by tradition worms,
we grew quickly
transplanted on alien soils
exchanging the darkness of solid roots
for the brief green of spring.

This is our inheritance then:
defeat and its accompanying despair
uniting us with others
shunned by victory.

This then is our forgetfulness:
our bandit selves
hijacking, striking where we can
in history's autumnal trail.
We grab at decoy flowers,
mirages of immutability
in the desolation of our loss.

But they return
angrily, in vindictive silence
the notes scribbled
on our hearts
by our hopeless ancestors.
They return
both as a promise and a threat.

Wedding

Women weep, sisters and mothers weep
Knowing what partings mean
Knowing the meaning of playing a part
Knowing the truth
Of distances, dreams and men.

Momentarily,
Mother becomes bride
Her first look at the past,
Her last look at the future.
In the mist of perfume and tears
The women wail
Mother embraces her child.

No man can comprehend
No man can cast asunder
That bond of partings and tears
That unites them,
Our sisters, our mothers.

Two Women

(1)

Pearl Sravanmutta
is over ninety now.
She prefers to cook her own meals
"Indian curries, not what they dish out
on meals on wheels."
She has no doctor
and feels dizzy crossing streets.
Her wiry hands wave about like sticks.
She dresses in a sari for the camera and smiles
She wants people to know she still has style.
Opening an old fridge she complains
"The rich are getting richer
and the poor poorer, Mrs Thatcher
has ruined this country."
She finds it hard to do things on her own.
The lads from the betting shop are nice;
They send someone to help her place her bets,
though her TV is going up the creek.
She likes to take a chance now and then
on an old horse, she says
there's nowhere these days to go for a dance.
Her photograph, taken years ago
in a Bond Street studio
her prize possession
faded now and grown old.
She loves hot Biryanis,
I'm told.

Two Women

(II)

Mrs Arif, from Turkey complains
barely moving her arthritic hands:
"I have no social worker."
Her wheelchair existence
supplemented by books in Turkish,
an old radio, a telephone and most important,
bottles of pain-killers.
"My son is a manager at Habitat"
She says ever so proudly
lifting up a photograph of her grand children,
"Of course, he has his own family now
And has little time for me"
But he does on occasion,
take her out to tea.
Her knotted twisted hands
remind her of her loss;
she used to embroider costumes
for great theatre stars
when she came here via Cyprus
thirty years ago, before the war.
Her fourth floor flat
is suitably adapted
for disabled tenants,
but there's no lift
so she cannot venture out too often.
"I only came here because of my son"
she says, with a glint in her eyes.

Refugee

The doors are locked upon our hearts
Like frightened birds our dreams have taken flight
Through neon mists the train departs
And a fearful silence lingers in the night

There is no music, no disguise
To hide behind and find a way to home
No point in waiting for the sun to rise
No option left except to learn to roam

Break off the sorrow from the pain
the one that lasts a moment, the other more prolonged
Take stock of what is lost and what is gained
and wonder to whom victory belonged.

So farewell friends, companions and to love
more beautiful than all the world can give
My bleeding words my wounded dove
We'll kill our hearts so we can live!

Candle

My lips burn black
whenever I speak.
My eyes drip down
with tears and congeal.
Though I am full of light
my voice is heard through darkness.
My language is the shadow
of other beings.
My song is the breeze
gently playing.

When I am alone, 1 am mute.

Outside My Window

Outside my window
the night waits for me.
She sends out dreams
and stars to lure me,
but the dreams fall
dead against the window pane,
and the disappointed stars
sink back into its mouth.

She comes closer to the window
as the lights go out
and puts her belly
right against the glass.
I look at night, so dark and vast
as a woman's hips are
when held close,
vast, embracing
circumscribing all the senses.

I open the window to touch her
but she moves further from my reach,
eagerly I move as the darkness moves
till at last we reach the edge
of the world.
And then, with a gende push,
I encounter the morning.

Morning Star

Is it a splinter
in your eye, lone star
that makes you blink?

Or is it the teardrop
in my eye
that makes you dwindle?

Some call this night,
some call it dawn;
and wedged in between
is the sky
and my lost dream.

Sitar Player

The still boat on the river,
the tall grass
through which she moves and floats away,
carried by the currents
of fingertips...

She steps on a thorn
and her body shudders
and bends towards her feet;
your fingers biting
into the strings
bleed out a story of love.

And the poverty of roses!

As a sudden breeze
catches the edge of her dress
and enrhythms
the cold stillness of a tree,
the dance begins
in the restless strings
straining against their voices
again and again;
and the fingers no longer yours
but the dancing girl's

gone out across the river...

A boat drifts, a girl wanders,
the sound of water,
the sound of grass,
the sound of fingers bleeding

in the rebellion of strings!

Blind Love

Pretending to be blind
is an art itself;
and he had practised well.
The way he would keep his eyes wide open
and act as if he saw nothing...

And she was at an age
when beautiful women become nai've
out of boredom,
open to new experiences,
inexperienced men, blind men...

Their meeting was without pretence;
the blindness of one
concealed the hypocrisy of the other.
Their parting was clear
as a blind man's darkness,
as a beautiful woman's face.

Suicide

A bird sat on a green branch
                          singing.
A bird sat with its beak against
                               its breast.
A bird sat with its beak
                    lost in its feathers.
A bird sat bleeding red flowers
                          from its breast.
A bird sat on a tree
                eating its own heart,
splattering leaves with red stars.
A bird sat near evening on a tree.
A bird fell from a tree
                leaving blood heavy leaves,
and a branch stretching
                into the darkest night.

No Comment

There was a time when words
like love and hate, came easily to me
Like so many faces they jostled
smudged and edged out spaces
from the page, pried out furtive sounds
from their silent hiding places
and made a song and dance
about the way the world was made.

Now that so much has been granted
voices, signs and icons all abound
I feel a desperate silence all around
Ambiguities increase with every doubt
The silence grows however much we shout.

So I must learn to contemplate
Poetry on a stubborn blank screen
To pixilate it with phantom loves
Or smudge it once again with hate
Is, to say the least, obscene.

From Stars:

Freedom

They crawled out slowly
from their caves,
silver spiders.
The night held them
static in its net
of black jelly.
When the earth turned
                        the sun
melted the night's blackness.
The stars fell over
the edge
                        and we were freed
from our enslavement.

Dreaming Stars

The stars came out
one night without
their faces.
They had no eyes
nor spoke to us
through their dark lips.
A crippled shadow
wept over the clouds
where the moon might have been.
They said in the village that a
woman lost her child.
When the sun came out
we discovered the unity
of faceless dreamers.

Falling Stars

When the star fell
all eyes turned upwards.
Its silver signature
tore the darkness,
a visual scream
in the silence of night,
an infant torn from
the mother's arms
to briefly cry its separation.
When we found its charred remains,
we could not believe it,
so small, so lightless,
the meteorite
that had held us in awe.

Broken Star

The gnarled
skeleton of the star
haunted the night's eye.
They looked at it
and hid in light
To drown
the sorrow of their dream.
They buried the heap
Of twisted silver light
Into the gaping hole
Of their tears.
But each night it
Reappeared
Silently upon them
And subverted their love-making

Alien Star

The alien star
shone in the corner
of the sky
with its strange light.
It stood there
clumsily
in the midst
of collapsing giants.
Time wove a rainbow blanket
around his waist;
history chained him
to another galaxy.
At night
he stole a smile
and in the day
when no other stars
could see him
he wept.
Through the alien
blankncss, his dusty tears fell
to where a new galaxy
was burning
made of millions
of fragments
of alien stars.

Black Star

It was the black star
in a silver sky,
a brilliant absence.
It was the shadow
of the sun
but at night it became all space.
The night belonged
to the black star
but the silver stars
stood out smiling
stealing the show.
They did not know
how many had lost their way
in the laughter
of the black star.

The Sun is Your Flower

The sun is your flower
It turns where you go
My dark-haired, dark-eyed, darkest love
In the deeps of your sighs
so many summers whisper.
My heart beats
like a tabla,
a *gat* played
by pagan musicians.
1 a supplicant
at your door,
Give me the honey
of forgetfulness
So I can love no more!

Ghazal

When you come to meet me
I don't know what happens
to my senses.
I wonder if your coming
was only an illusion.

Why do you embarrass me
with presents of flowers?
Throw a stone at me;
I am a madman since I saw you.

Why imprison me
in this city, why tie me down with civility?
I am a lover of *Leila*
my home is the wilderness.

Hide those burning lips
with the dark curtains of your hair,
the sparks from your smile
will kill this moth.

O Saqi do not give me the wine of Love
with such abundance.
1 fear the glass will burst
with the heat!

I Saw You Dancing

I saw you dancing
I saw
the breeze scatter
from your fingertips.
1 saw your mouth
blossoming
from your face.
I saw your hair
turning into waves
and crashing
against the barriers of my mind.
So enchanting was your presence
that I could not take my eyes
from your breasts.
I do not remember
seeing your legs, the legs
that were the fulcrum of the dance.
I saw your eyes staring
through the forest of my dreams
and flash and disappear
as I turned my head.
All this I saw
and you insist
that you were standing still.

Like the Moon

Like the moon
dispersing darkness
with its light
your smile also
has a darker side.
And I like a wave
caught in that strange
magic reach upwards
and fall.
Through the night sky
of my being
you pass by
like a satellite
brightening and darkening
my heart.

Song

How many times do we have to part
before we can be friends
How many times do we have to meet
before our love can end.

My hands tied up
 with a neat bouquet
fresh flowers bought
as after thought
of better days.

My lips can feel
that distant kiss
My eyes replay
your falling tears,
What can I say?

1 force a smile
at your hello
I'll stay a while
and then I'll go
I cannot stay?

How many times do we have to part
before our love can end
How many times do we have to meet
before we can be friends.

Note: This poem was inspired by Faiz Ahmad Faiz's 'Ham ke Thabre Ajnabi'

Prevention of Terrorism

It is not good to attack other people
Because they will attack you.

It is not good to bash other people
Because they will bash you.

It is not good to whack other people
Because they will whack you.

It is not good to clobber other people
Because they will clobber you.

It is not good to bomb other people
Because they will bomb you.

It is not good to murder other people
Because they will murder you.

We have bombed innocent people
They have bombed innocent people

It is not good to terrorise other people
Because they will terrorise you.

What's it All About?

It is about
Baghdad
Basra
Fallujah
Abu Ghraib
Guantanamo

It is about
Oil
Money
Contracts
Power

It is about
Ramallah
Jerusalem
Jenine,
Jericho

It is about
Tanks
Gunships
Occupation
It is about
100,000 dead
Cities Wasted

It is about
Tiny coffins lined up
Upon an Afghan hillside
It is about naked men piled up

Like dead meat.
It is about hooded prisoners
Chained to a wall.

It is about
Mothers, widows
Limbless orphans
Bombed from the sky
Not knowing why.
It is about
Wedding parties
Torn to shreds with missiles

It is about collateral damage
Running into thousands
It is about
War criminals
Wielding death.

It is about
Assassination
Humiliation
Exclusion
Impotence

It's not about
Our Way of Life

BUT IT DOESN'T MAKE IT RIGHT.

8th July 2005

A Child's Prayer

My hopes and dreams emerge as a prayer on my lips:
O Lord, make my life a candle bright
From whose glow the darkness is dispersed
And the world is brightened by its shining light.
Through me my nation should find dignity
As a garden is admired by a flower's beauty.
Like a moth entranced by the light of knowledge may I be
In love with learning, toil, fanciful and free.
May 1 live to serve the poor, the humble and the meek
To love the afflicted, infirm, old and weak.
Protect me from evil ways O Lord above
Guide me on the path of Goodness, Peace and Love.

Translated from Urdu of Dr Mohammad Iqbal

WORD ✪ POWER BOOKS

**Revolutionary Witticisms of
Colin Fox, Rosie Kane and
Carolyn Leckie MSPs**

Gregor Gall
ISBN 0-9549185-0-9

'"Politicians'witticisms' is one of the great oxymorons
of our time. It ranks alongside 'UN peacekeepers' and
'Channel Five News'. When an elected member cracks
a funny, it is normally heavily penned by various party
political comedians. It is fortunate then that the SSP
can't afford to pay for proper script writers and have
to rely on their own one liners. Politicians, it has to be
said, do make me laugh but it is quite refreshing to
read a politician's words and laugh because they
intended you too."

Mark Thomas
Comedian, writer and political activist.